DIVORCING NORMAL

Chasing After Eden

By
PROPHET TIFFANY EALY

Copyright 2022 © by Tiffany Ealy
All Rights Reserved

ISBN: 978-0-578-26865-1

LCCN 2022915380

This book is protected by copyright laws in the United States of America. This book may not be reprinted of copied for commercial use or commercial gains.
Scripture notations are taken from the Holy Bible. (Different Versions) I am not a counselor and this book is intended to bring truth and knowledge of God's word. All rights are reserved under copyright law. Contents of this book/Cover shall not be reproduced in part or in any form without written permission by the author/publisher of the book.

Empac Publishing Company
Po Box 1192
Fresno, TX 77545
tiffanyealyspeaks@gmail.com

Dedication

Always thankful to God, my wonderful husband, children, in-laws, family, fans, and true friends!

This book is dedicated to my father the late Anthony G. Pierre Sr. what you were unable to carry out on the Earth, I am carrying the torch to fulfill God's purpose. Thankful to every mentor, prophet and tutor that God has sent along the way to ensure I continue on the right pathway. Each of us has special angels I call them that are assigned to us to push, thrust, and influence our lives to bring us to another level. I know that I am a Repairer of The Breach, for my family and others. I am called to tear down, build up and assist in restoring what the enemy has attempted to steal. We have a full inheritance that belongs to us and we shall recover all!

We are unstoppable when we partner with the only, "Unlimited God!"

We Shall Recover All, We Shall See God's Fulfillment In Our Lives!

Autographs

Your Value, Worth & Destiny IS Written By God, Not Man!
You Are Meant to Soar, Rise, & Walk In A Truth!
You Are An Inheritor, Heir, & Truly Powerful!

TIFFANY EALY

#TESpeaks

Table of Contents

PHASE I: DIVORCING NORMAL INTRO

Introduction	1
Wilderness	6
Cast It Down	12
Limiting Beliefs	16
Negative Words	20
Un-Forgiveness	24
Dry Bones	33
Damaged Goods	37

PHASE II: CHASING EDEN

Kingdom	42
Tithing	46
Birthing	50
The Torch	54
Favor	59
Rainbows Coming Now	63
Success	67
The Promise	70
Who Am I	77

PHASE I
Divorcing Normal Intro

Introduction

Today, As I begin to write this book, I ponder on the state of our world, the church, our community and families. Most of us have accepted Jesus Christ as Lord. We have been in church all of our lives, but we sat there without an understanding of truth and knowledge of true identity and authority. The question is, did we change, grow, and were we in church homes that were alive and performing miracles? Oftentimes, we sat in the pew and we didn't grow and we sat there just eating crumbs and hearing the same word over and over again. When we are saved and we receive salvation in Christ, we first accept Christ through faith and believe that Christ exists. Salvation does not include just being saved, but it includes becoming wealthy, gaining wisdom, the Holy Spirit, deliverance, and operating in freedom. Then we can have the understanding that helps us to advance the Kingdom and walk in the principles of the Kingdom. When we are saved we have full access to our Brother and the inheritance of heaven. We are now under the new covenant where Jesus Christ is our intercessor in heaven, and we have all rights to the heavenly attributes. We should not just be eating crumbs in church, but we have to begin to understand our worth, value and true authority as Kings & Queens both spiritually and naturally. I think back to the traditions of our forefathers and parents who lived by what they were taught in tradition. Some curses stayed in our family line because they didn't know they existed nor how to break them. They saw the perversion, fornication, and addictions and other sin but we just accepted and went into survival mode. The word and Bible haven't changed but we believed in principles that we were taught and didn't learn truth and foundation. This is why so many things have to be untaught and relearned, so we can begin to move in authority and Kingdom. Having a two-family home the way God designed as husband and wife who are healed is important. The enemy before the beginning of time tried to attack families through violence, slavery and distorting our identity. Then tactics of abortion, poverty, violence, and word curses attacked our family even more. The enemy does not want our marriages to succeed and operate in authority, love and power. As long as we accept perversion, fornication, and other sins and don't become the curse breakers, we live under our divine inheritance. We receive only the entertainment and a temporary fix. We are called to advance the seven mountains of the Earth and have influence. Each of us is called to different mountains which are ministry, education, media/communications, entertainment, government, business, and family. We are all called to influence one or more mountains in the world. We are called to utilize our anointing to break yokes and destroy the wrong foundations while bringing forth foundations that will produce fruit and a harvest. We are called to produce, multiply, and subdue the Earth. We are called to bring down heaven on Earth and see wonders.

The definition of the word normal says in the Oxford, to conform to standards that are usual, typical or expected. Normal adjectives that we see

INTRODUCTION

would be typical, average, and standard. God has not created us as normal beings, but we are created as spiritual beings in His image. If we are created in the image of Christ, we are created to be supernatural beings that have authority, power, and spiritual insight that give us divine advantage over the world. To walk in the Supernatural, the definition describes that there is some force beyond science that is in control; God, spirit, and we depart from normal and appear to transcend the laws of nature. When we walk in the Supernatural, we are walking in Kingdom Law; and that law is above the natural law. The Supernatural can't be traced. We are made to do significant things, and the word says that greater works will be done through Him if we believe in Him. (John 14:12) I don't know about you, but I want everything that God has for me and my family. I remember receiving a prophecy and the prophet said that there are lines of people waiting for you to walk in destiny. I pondered on that word, and I began to think about those assigned to me that need what I have to move forward in their purpose. Then I had a dream; in the dream, God showed me that I was in a store where people were in line waiting to check out. I was behind the counter and I was unlocking the security mechanism off their purchases. They could not move forward with the purchase until the lock was removed. God said those assigned to you can't move forward in destiny until they connect with you to be unlocked. That was profound, I certainly didn't want to hold up anyone's progress. I know how it feels to be stuck, stagnant and confused and cry out to God for help. This book is about leaving behind everything that does not belong to us. The sickness, poverty, hurt, pain, trauma, rejection, stagnation, delay, unforgiveness, unbelief and of course, generational curses. These things are not our portion. Jesus already died on the cross and shed blood so that we can live in freedom and out of darkness. The same power that raised Jesus Christ from the dead lives in us. (Romans 8:11) That means that we have full access from the Father to break curses and walk in authority. We are fully equipped for the purpose we are created to walk in. The problem is that many of our gifts within lie dormant, dreams have died, and we carry too many burdens. We have weight in the spirit but we don't use it and get tired of waiting in the natural. Today, we are not accepting normal, but striving to see heaven come to Earth in our lives. We cancel normal, and we decree that Eden is our portion. What belongs to us shall come forth and manifest now.

> *"So I took them out of the land of Egypt and brought them into the wilderness"*
>
> EZEKIEL 20:10

Wilderness

Most of us are aware of the story in Exodus where Moses leads the Israelites who wandered in the wilderness for 40 years. This story is an important story about walking in the wilderness and being misled and mistreated for years. The Israelites were mistreated, injured and damaged by the Egyptian bondage. When Moses was appointed to lead them out, they had to first be convinced that they could inherit the land. Their plight also lasted longer than it should because of disobedience, unbelief and the failure to trust in God. They disobeyed an important command that they should not have any other gods. They constructed a statue and began to worship the statue. Their mindset had been enslaved that they had disbelief that they could take the land. The ones that had unbelief had to be killed off so the others could take the land with Joshua. God performed miracles on their journey and met their needs of food and water, but they still failed to trust God. The wilderness plight is an intense experience of stagnation, delay, fear, isolation, danger, and deliverance. The wilderness as we see can be overcome, but we must be obedient and believe in the Father and move in Kingdom principles. Don't judge what season

WILDERNESS

you are in or a person is in because everyone has a pit or wilderness season. This season is temporary, for your next.

Each of us will have a wilderness situation where we feel lonely, self-doubt, despair and knocked down by life. In order for us to reach the mountain top, we have to first experience our pit experience. This is different for each of us, and the length of time is as well different. In the wilderness is where we are tested, trained, refined, built, restored, renewed and set free. When we are in the wilderness, we feel we have no one but God. This is a time when we seek God like no other. No one can help us but God. The wilderness is hard and harsh on us just like the experience with the Israelites. The wilderness is a place that we certainly don't want to stay. When we go through the wilderness, we also can delay our breakthrough by unbelief and not being attentive to the Holy Spirit. The wilderness is certainly not meant to be permanent but only temporary. As in the scripture, in Exodus, we saw that the Israelites grumbled and complained and God still provided over and over. God is still the same God during the wilderness and on the mountain. Sometimes we feel like He has left us because we can't feel Him moving on our behalf. We begin to feel stuck and stagnant. His word says that He shall never leave us nor forsake us. He is still there but sometimes the teacher is also silent but working behind the scenes for our good. It is so imperative that when we are in the wilderness, we listen and follow instructions. We should not follow our own leading and lose patience. Like the example in the Bible where Hagar was pregnant with Ishmael, this brought confusion and consequences because of unbelief in God's ability to do what He said. God works in His timing, and we must believe and endure so we can see His hand and His fruit. The endurance produces purity, and belief in us. When we fail to believe and listen, we fall to our own will and abilities.

I can remember a time when I was in what I call my pit situation. I felt like I was praying, believing and fasting and the doors were still closed. I was trying my hardest to stay upbeat, but I was losing momentum and it was getting hard. I was looking for God to work on my behalf. When finally, I changed my prayer. I asked God what I am supposed to be doing now. He then began to speak to me and brought His prophets with a word of life. He told me that I had been disobedient to write my book and publish it. I wanted Him to open the door for a job, but I was sitting on my gifts and what was in my hands. I had to repent and go forward with His instruction. This caused me to have a fire again to go forth and move forward. I also realized that in the wilderness, I was made stronger and healed from some insecurities that were a stronghold in my life. I began to praise God because I knew the wilderness was necessary, yet hard. I was confident that now was the time to be obedient to His plan, and not my own plan. For so long, I had tried to do it my way. Well, it was time to do it the right way. Our rehearsal of the problem and not looking to the promise can also keep us stranded. We must look ahead and not back to what was before. God says that when we go into the wilderness, it is an announcement of a new season. That new season comes forth after you have encountered the pit. The pit is not meant to harm you, but to propel and stretch you forward. It is a place of surrender to fully accept and yield to His plan. When you are disturbed in your present, God is ready to increase and improve the now!

"When You Feel You Are In A Place of Darkness; You Are Actually In A Place of Planting!" D Ealy

The Umbrella

Imagine you are carrying an umbrella and it is raining hard. You have a strong umbrella that you are holding steady. God and His angels are above your head protecting you and interceding on your behalf. A word of prophecy has just been spoken and you are strong in your faith. Then a principality of darkness tries to invade your space. The principality comes to try and deter, kill and destroy the prophetic word. Your umbrella is shifted just a little and you are now in an experience of warfare. This is the time when you have to stand on the word of God so that heaven is activated and you are not moved. It is a time to continue to seek God 1st in all things. The word says that when the enemy comes, God will raise a higher standard against the enemy on your behalf. We must trust in the God we serve because nothing can withstand His word. The promise shall come to pass if we believe, trust and activate His word over our lives. God should always be our center and cornerstone during the wilderness and in good times. We must fully seek the Father at all times. Sometimes more wilderness tests are sent just to get our attention and for us to know His will for our lives. We always have a choice to move with Him or not. Your umbrella will hold steady and not be overtaken if we stay in His word, utilize His word, and move in obedience. Remember that you are built and equipped for the wilderness and the mountain top. You are always backed by heaven and the angels assigned to you. We access heaven with our voice and His word shall keep us strong and steady. God is our center, and nothing can stand against Him. We shall not fail because God is for us and with us. When we are holding steady, we have to speak, then see the promise so we can believe His revelation. Faith is heaven's currency that guarantees our promise when we believe.

Weapons

The Armor of God
Prayer strategies for your situation
Fasting
Praying in The Spirit
Command the Angels
Praise & Worship
Testimony of what God did last time
Agreement
Sit in Presence of God

The Wilderness

We are made Strong
Birthing Place
Teaching (Learn What You Need)
Testing
Refined
Delivered
Patience Produced
Shows You, & Who God Is
Necessary to Grow
Announcement Of a New Season
Strategy Learned
Built
Surrender

"We destroy arguments and every lofty opinion raised against the knowledge of God, take every thought captive to obey Christ"

2 CORINTHIANS 10:5

Cast It Down

In Genesis, at the beginning, man was created in God's image. Man didn't begin to breathe until the Father gave breath into man's nostrils. In order for man to completely live, he must have breath (wind). In order for the things in our lives to live, we must speak life into them, because without the spoken word, they will die. Our blessing is created in heaven and is ready to be released from heaven. When we receive a word of prophecy, it is detailing and rehearsing what is ready to come down from heaven. We must work the word and also speak life over the word so it can live. We must also move in obedience which allows our faith to go forth. God needs us to activate His plans on Earth. We need God's truth, wisdom, and the authority that belongs to us to live a Kingdom life. Negative emotions and words must be cast down and not allowed to attach to us. We must continue to speak God's word even when the situation seems dim. We are responsible to shut off and protect the gifts, legacy and inheritance that God has placed inside of us. When things do not line up with His word, they should be cast down and bound. When we allow wrong words to attach to us, it will produce what was spoken. This is why we see negative occurrences happen in our life. We must constantly cast down the wrong imaginations, words, and attachments.

We have the authority to change the station of our minds. When we think negatively, we bring forth negative things. We also bring the wrong vibe to us and slow down what belongs to us. This is the reason why the word says our mind needs to be renewed daily. We have so many thoughts that come to us and not all of them are good thoughts. We must continuously cast down what does not belong to us. For example, think of a time when something bad occurred to you. When this occurred, did you think about the occurrence over and over again and rehearse it in your mind? We are probably all responsible for doing this in our lives. We must change the station and begin to speak what God says. What we rehearse more is what we will receive. Sometimes it may be hard to even pray, but we must activate our tongues and speak in the spirit. We must continue to cast down the wrong thoughts and we must combat the old thoughts with the word of God. We can also get with like-minded individuals to pray for us. We know that the Bible says there is power in agreement and God is with us.

Cast down the wrong imaginations, and we must begin to trust God's word. The more we rehearse what God says, the more we believe God. When we praise God in the middle of the situation, that shows God we are trusting Him. When we speak His Word, we are using the word as a weapon against the enemy. We know that we fight against principalities and not humans. The word of God is a major weapon to fight the enemy. We can't activate what belongs to us in heaven without using our voice to cast down wrong imaginations and speak the word of God. Kingdom is voice-activated. We also have angels in the heavens that are waiting on us so God can command them on our behalf. Cast down what doesn't belong and prophesy into existence God's promises. It tells us in His word that He is not a man that He should lie. His perfect promises are true and perfect and they shall come to pass. We must believe, stand, and act.

Our Minds

Do not conform to the pattern of this world, but be transformed by the renewing of your mind

ROMANS 12:2 NIV

The biggest war we face now is in our minds. The inner me can be another enemy if we let it. Instead of speaking ourselves into our destiny, we speak ourselves out of moving in destiny. We question ourselves, and not only that, we also question what God said. Not only do we not believe what He said, but we don't trust in who we were created to be. When we question the gifts within us, we are questioning the creator who made us. He made us with a purpose that was ordained before we were an embryo. The full book of our daily life is written in heaven, but we must know what it contains. We place a limit on our Father when we have limiting thoughts of ourselves. We truly have to change our thoughts to concentrate on heaven's will for our lives. We can't be moved by our emotions because they will steer us wrong. We will not feel like doing what we need to do. For example, you may not feel like going to work, but you know you have to in order to get a paycheck. We have to move beyond our feelings and activate our minds. That is a big reason why we must renew our minds on a daily basis. Some things come and get us off track of what we should be doing. We must not allow these things to affect us from moving and pushing ahead. Yes, it is normal to have wrong thoughts at times, but we need to cast the thoughts down. We must decree God's word over our minds and activate positivity over our minds. When we limit ourselves, we are limiting God who is within us. Take the limits off, speak life over your thoughts and mind daily, and go forth knowing you are made to win. You have the mind of Christ within, and your mind was created by the Elohim. Follow the manufacturer's instructions and you will win for sure. The mind is a powerful place and we first have to get instructions from the mind to move forward. The mind controls the body. For example, when a person is sick with Alzheimer's, they are limited in thinking, movement, and remembering because the mind is not being renewed but failing. Our thoughts are created in the mind and our imagination must think it before we believe and act on it. We have to dream again and our dreams need to manifest in our minds so we can move in them. I decree that the thoughts of our mind shall correlate with what heaven says about us. We have to hold a supernatural mind in this natural world. Our minds must think big and go higher so we can go to that place.

Limiting Beliefs

Each of us was given a measure of God's faith according to who we are. In the word, it talks about the faith of a mustard seed which is so small, but the thing about a mustard seed is that if it is watered, it grows in size tremendously. We are babies in Christ and as we grow in the word of God and kingdom principles, we grow in our faith. We are able to walk in greater faith as we overcome and are led by God. We become grounded in our faith and able to believe and trust. We oftentimes carry limiting beliefs. We believe what man who didn't create us has said instead of what God says. We talk ourselves out of the blessing instead of into the blessing. Why? Because fear and unbelief exist. We all have been there where we let fear get the best of us. We think small and our unbelief takes over our minds. We do have faith but unbelief hides our faith and we operate from fear instead of faith. The limitations we place on ourselves restrict us from moving forward. Of course, the enemy wants us to be limited because he does not want us to be in unity in our homes, marriages and life itself. If the enemy can cause fear and incite fear in us, we will be stagnant and muted in our life. This is also important to know that we must again cast down the thoughts that hinder our progress and cause us to think small.

LIMITING BELIEFS

We can't move in a larger capacity if we still think small. Small can take over our lives because of generational thoughts and curses as well. We don't think bigger because we have not seen it happen to anyone. Again, someone may have come to us with words of offense and spoke down to us and told us lies. This is why it is important to know who we are. When we know who we are, no one can define us and limit our thoughts. To limit someone is to place a boundary on something and it only goes to a certain level. We serve a limitless God and we must know that we are fully equipped to move in our gifts and talents.

The Problems of the world and our everyday issues can bring strife and stress. Stress can certainly take over our lives and cause sickness and pain. It gets worse because we rehearse the problem we are going through over and over. God says we should cast our cares on Him and the word. When we don't cast them on Him, we carry extra heavy baggage that was not meant for us to carry. We will have stress in life but we can also take hold of God's peace. When we walk in peace, we know that we have God's word to combat the storm and that He will move on our behalf. When someone or something does something to us we have to meditate on the word first. We must take our hurt and pain to the Most High. We can't allow the circumstance to overtake us and move us. We must allow the word of God to guide us, comfort us and direct our paths. Worry and stress are certainly not of God and both are demonic attacks.

We certainly have all experienced setbacks and delays in our lives. This can cause worry because we feel stuck. It is not that we won't go through, but who we access while going through is important. We must diligently seek the one who has the answer for us. I remember looking for a job again. It seemed like no door was opening and I knew I was qualified and educated.

DIVORCING NORMAL, CHASING EDEN

As I began to get discouraged, I was led to pray a different prayer. I began to ask God, What am I supposed to be doing now?" He responded and told me that I was to get my first book out and that I was sitting on my talents and gifts. It made me reevaluate things and went back and did what He said. Sometimes we have received the instruction, but we fail to follow the instruction because we have our own plan. I had pretty much completed the book, but I had not moved because of fear and other things. Today, remember that fear will keep you down if you let it. You can't operate in your gifts if you don't try and move. How can we worry when we fail to listen. I certainly had to repent to the Father because I had operated in sin because of my disobedience at the time. We must remember that being comfortable will not push us where we are headed. We must move out of our comfort zone so we can be stretched into purpose. We must today cancel worry, stress, strife and all the demonic attacks that are causing delays in our lives. They are not of God, and they are not our portion. Cast down the worry and rebuke it over your life. It is not your portion. Allow neither yourself nor others to limit what God has already ordained and approved.

"The tongue has power of life and death, and those that love to talk will reap the consequences"

PROVERBS 18:21 NLT

Negative Words

We need to know that our words create and cause life or death. I am big on words because I look at how words have affected so many people including myself. I can remember speaking to someone who said they were called ugly. This stigma stayed with them and they felt ugly even as an adult. Then we also have children and the rejection we experience if not dealt with follows our children as well. Negative words can have an impact that delays and attempts to steal destiny. When negative words attach to our lives, we begin to live below God's standard for our life. We believe what others say instead of what God says. I know oftentimes, when we get emotional about something or in an argument, words are released and hurt and damage occur. We must remember each seed produces after its own kind. When we speak negatively about someone and others, we bring that to us, and we stagnate others as well. We have to constantly monitor our words, so we won't hinder our lives or others. When something goes wrong for example, and you say I can't catch a break, you just spoke that negative word and brought more of the same. We must also look and see why the negative patterns are happening. Oftentimes, the negative things come from our own mouths, others or generational curses

NEGATIVE WORDS

as well. We must be fully aware of the words that we speak; even the jokes we make are words that create. Remember, heaven is voice-activated by our words. The world was created by the words of God " Let there be". Many times, we spoke and it came to pass. You don't have to accept anyone's negative words spoken against your life. Remember to cast it down immediately. The words and the comments do not belong to you. If it does not line up with God's word, it is not for you. What God says about you matters to you and defines who you are. We must be careful not to let man define us because it places control on us and our destiny. Remember to rebuke the wrong, and replace it with the right words.

I recall that in my first book, I mentioned this. I was sitting in a leadership training session for my new position. This was a day on which I felt really bad and a little under the weather. I was there but not fully there. The presenter asked us who we had met in our lives that caused a great impact. He wanted to know what greats we had encountered in our life. I was pondering the question over and over, but I wasn't sure of my answer. Many had spoken of great leaders that had truly changed their life and perspective. He got to me and I said, " I haven't met any greats but I am destined for greatness." I spoke life over myself and the class chuckled, but I knew that my destiny had greatness attached to it. Today, I have met many great Apostles and Prophets who God has used to motivate, empower and impact my life. I probably would have answered differently and spoke of one of my encounters with a great, but I am still certainly destined for greatness." I am writing this book today because of the greatness and the gifts God has placed in me. Remember to create life with your words and don't limit who you are. Negative words will produce a negative outcome. Speak not what you see in your life, but what God says and can be. We can't get caught in seeing through worldly things, but we have to have a spiritual lens that changes our words. One word can activate and change your current situation and current position. Remember your position won't change when you think and act negatively. Negativity is not of God and not your portion. Cancel today, the wrong words, wrong attitude, wrong perspective, and wrong thoughts. You are what God says, and not what man says.

"Your Word is Your Judge, Your Words Create So As You Speak So Shall It Be!"

"For if you forgive your enemy their trespasses, your heavenly father will also forgive you, but if you don't forgive others their trespasses, neither will your father forgive you"

MATTHEW 6:14-15

Un-Forgiveness

Oftentimes, we wonder why someone is sick, and they have prayed and fasted but nothing happened. That person may be holding on to unforgiveness from the past and has not forgiven. I recall a time when a family member spoke about a situation that happened 30 years ago, and they had not let it go. This was an example where they had held onto the unforgiveness over a long period of time. This was certainly not a healthy situation. When we feel that we have been wronged, and we feel rejected, we must go to God. We have to seek our Father who is a healer and still heals. We must activate our healing by speaking scriptures, and also forgiving others when we feel wronged. Forgiveness is certainly not always easy. It is hard because when someone you love injures you, it feels like a physical injury. There is emotional and physical pain involved. God forgives us when we repent and turn from our wicked ways, and He expects us to forgive others. The forgiveness of others has to go forth so we can also be forgiven by our Father. We must trust the Father that He will judge what has been done to us.

UN-FORGIVENESS

Things happen in our life where someone or something has caused us to feel rejected or injured. This pain on the inside of us is like physical pain, and it must be healed and dealt with. This is another way that the enemy tries to deter us from our future. When we don't forgive those that have wronged us, it is sin, and we are bound. When we begin to also rehearse the occurrence, the unforgiveness continues to grow and get larger. The pain places a hole in our heart that it is enlarged. If not dealt with, we will certainly begin to feel heaviness, sickness, delay and other things that hinder our progress in life. We must go to the father and open our hearts to repent and ask God to help us forgive. Forgiveness is not to say that we were not wronged, but it is to let go of the hurt and pain. We do not have to reconnect with that but we must love them and forgive. We must learn from the mistakes and the lesson of the occurrence. The past must be looked at as a lesson and a test. We must look forward to the promise that is ahead and greater than the injury.

The Father says that He is the judge. He sees the things that others do to us and how they have treated us. This is an opportunity for us to forgive and place the problem at the altar and give it to God. The things that we should have in our life should resemble heaven. Our lives should reflect all the things God has for us in the heavenly realm. Oftentimes, we hold on to unforgiveness, trauma, pain and rejection and our life that brings forth depression, stagnation, and other things that resemble the enemy's plan. God's plan is for us to walk in the fullness of potential and greatness He created for His children. His plan is divine and includes freedom, wholeness and every attribute of heaven. We must let go of the unforgiveness and not allow others or ourself to be held hostage by the enemy. We must go forth in following God's way of forgiveness.

It is not always easy because hurt people begin to hurt others. Many people are walking around hurt and carrying extra weight that doesn't belong to them. Forgiveness may be a process in our lives. It is vital for us to forgive and walk in freedom for ourselves. We can't allow anyone or anything to hold us hostage to our future. Our future is very important and our legacy depends on it as well. Forgiveness is our portion and it is possible. What if the person you didn't forgive dies tomorrow? We can't allow anything to hinder our progress or our promise. Forgive, let go, and you can certainly still love them from a distance. Forgiveness does not require you to reconcile, but it does require you to love. Forgiveness is possible and in our portion, we can cast our cares so our burden can be lighter through the father. Don't allow anyone who did not create you to stifle your destiny because of how they made you feel. You must operate at the standard of how God created you in forgiveness and love. Many people who I forgave I may not speak to on a regular basis, but I will pray for you and be cordial with you. To hate someone is to hate what God created. Many hurt people do things to us because they allow the enemy to use them. This is why we can't allow the enemy to use us and hold on to resentment and unforgiveness.

Traditions

> *Let no one be found among you who sacrifices their son or daughter in the fire, who practices divination or sorcery, interprets omens, engages in witchcraft, or casts spells, or who is a medium or spiritist or who consults the dead.*
>
> DEUTERONOMY 18:10 NLT

UN-FORGIVENESS

Anyone who does there things is detestable to the Lord; because of these same detestable practices the Lord your God will drive out.

DEUTERONOMY 18:12 NLT

Oftentimes, the sin of our forefathers and those that have come before us can hinder the next generation. When our generational line has opened doors to sin whether unknowingly or knowingly, this can cause major stagnation for the next generation. The previous generation may have dabbled in witchcraft, divination, idolatry, fornication and other things that open doors for the generations after to be cursed. The sins of our ancestors can be passed down from generation to generation this is why we must repent, and fast. Through fasting, praying and knowledge, we can tear down the demonic altars that are affecting our destiny and bloodline. When God begins to reveal to us what is in our bloodline, he provides the strategy and power to us to tear down the strongholds. God wants us to truly live in freedom and the prosperity of heaven on Earth. The word says we are in the world but not of this world. The world has many evil principalities that come up against our destiny. We have an eternal high priest in heaven named Jesus Christ who intercedes for us, The Holy Spirit, as well as angels assigned. We must utilize the voice and the power of God within us to break down the forces of evil that try to take us down. We are victorious, prosperous and conquerors because we hold authority in the Spiritual realm.

Many people in our family belong to Christ and have accepted salvation. Salvation is just the beginning of the process. We have acknowledged Christ, but there is also a sin that has entered our lives in many ways. In order for us to fully be free, the curses have to be broken. The demonic oppression can be broken by the power of God. Once God makes us aware of the curses, we are responsible for our family line and breaking those curses. It requires the curses to be broken so we can activate the inheritance of our family line. Many spoils have been lost and stolen by the enemy and held up. Even those that have had an abortion, this is a curse that has to be broken because it can produce barrenness and excruciating pain. Also, witchcraft that was practiced in the family, the curses are passed down and open a demonic altar and allow the enemy to come in. For example, my family, including me, grew up Catholic. In the Catholic faith, they worship saints and statues which is a part of idolatry. In God's word, He speaks of not worshipping any gods besides him. For God is a jealous God. In the new age, many things are accepted as being ok and it is not. Horoscopes, mediums, tarots, sage, witchcraft, etc are not things that are of God. When anyone dabbles in these things, they are opening doors to the demonic realm. These things have to be denounced and rebuked over your family line because they can affect generations to come. The open doors that were opened before our time frame can still affect us and our family generations to come. This is why they must be broken. The open doors can cause poverty, stagnation, sickness, premature death, barrenness, and other things that are not ordained by our Father. Our Father intends for us to live a life that is filled with generational blessings and inheritance of every Kingdom attribute that belongs to us.

Tradition can be good and sometimes it can be detrimental to us. Poverty is not just a state but also a mindset. It stifles our abundance to move forward in our life. It keeps us in a place of lack and deficiency. No matter what your experience is, our Father has called us to be rich and has placed gifts in us to produce wealth in our hands. It is not our portion to live below our values. Faith is a currency of heaven that helps to bring forth our portion. We must be careful to follow the truth and not the traditions that mean us no good. For example, many eat black-eyed peas for New Year. This tradition has been passed down for many years. The tradition actually comes from the slaves eating the staple of beans because this is what was available for nourishment. This has nothing to do with wealth or moving into greater. We must know where traditions come from and research why. This is why many generations have experienced curses in the family line. We see the patterns that have attacked our family, but we do nothing and receive more of the same. It is time for us to live as God has ordained us to live. We must seek truth and walk in truth so that our legacy is blessed and shall prosper.

In our family line, most of our family members are Catholic because their parents were Catholic. I recall as a child my dad taking a step and wanting to learn and be under a different denomination. His best friend was the pastor of a Baptist Church, and he joined the church and left the Catholic denomination. This was looked upon as if he had sinned against God. My mother and other family members didn't want to accept him changing from the Catholic faith. What should have happened is that we went to the new church as a family and became members of his new church. We actually went to church with my mom mostly and we also visited with my dad at times. This was a division in our household. My mom was in the Catholic faith under rules and idolatry, and we were hearing two different words like there is more than one God. Denominations are basically religion and are governed by man-made rules. It is not of God. There is one universal God that is all and created all. We are all spiritual beings led by one God who is King of the Kingdom. Jesus Christ came to share the good news of the laws about living under the Kingdom. Many dead churches in our society are only teaching religion and not Kingdom. Many are surviving and wishing and not living a Kingdom life. It is time for the church to go into revival mode where Kingdom principles are taught and caught. We need to begin to know how to access heaven with our voice and move in obedience and favor with the father. We perish as the word says for lack of knowledge. Many don't know how to walk in kingdom principles. We don't understand how to pray, fast, and warfare and begin to see miracles and signs follow us. In the word, it said greater works will we do, but if we don't know kingdom, we can't see miracles, healings and people being transformed. Our life on Earth is to resemble heaven and where we transform and look like Jesus daily. We should see the church reflect unity and all the gifts operating to bring forth heaven to Earth. We all carry gifts from God but many gifts are still hidden. In order for us to activate Kingdom, our gifts must be activated and used for His glory. It's time for us to learn, acknowledge and walk in kingdom principles, not man's principles. We have all the benefits of the kingdom but if we don't know principles, we can't utilize them. It's time to let go of traditions that hinder us, and religion that stifles us because we need to see Eden on Earth. We are called to set atmospheres and walk in dominion here on Earth.

We are called not to be entertained and transformed by the world but called to resemble the Kingdom. Entertainment has become a place that many look to for guidance. Actors have become normal heroes. What about those that are living a life that is pleasing to God and saving souls. If we ask many people who they want to meet in life, many would provide the name of a star. My answer would be someone who truly is anointed, walks in purpose, and lives a life that stands on God's word. We have to be intentional about everything in our life. It seems normal in society to see homosexuality, transgender, open marriages, fornication, lust and other sins. This is not pleasing to our father. In the beginning, we were created male and female to reproduce, multiply and subdue on the Earth. Nothing has changed and our father does not make any mistakes. What was sin back then is still sin. Of course, we don't hate the people but we must hate the sin itself. We all have fallen short of something and we all have some type of sin in our lives. We must, however, learn to repent and turn away from sin. Our normal day should reflect God and seeking His will for us. Today, the answer is still God. Our Father still speaks to His Prophets, Apostles, and teachers of His word and whoever will seek Him. He is calling many of us to speak His word and be a light in a dark world. We are all called to be stewards of the gifts and the plans God has placed within us. We are called to bring lost souls to Christ. Many are lost and are fed by worldly things. Our blueprint for life doesn't come from the world but from above. God's word is still true and should live within us. We must strive to be better stewards of what we hear, see, and allow into our temples. For our temples belong to Christ and our spouse. What we place into us is what will come out and influence our daily choices and life. I always say that someone is assigned to be your answer, and you are assigned as an answer for many as well." I want to meet everyone in my life who is called to push me, influence me, and propel me forward in life. This allows us to live life fully and not just exist. We can't be compromised by the world because our children and many others depend on our walk. What we do in our life affects our legacy.

"You Are Not What Tradition Says, You Are A House of God!"

> *"Then he said to me, Speak a Prophetic message to these dry bones. Dry Bones, listen to the word of the Lord!"*
>
> EZEKIEL 37:4 NLT

Dry Bones

He asked me, "Son of man, Can these dry bones live?"

EZEKIEL 37:3

There are many things that our ancestors have prayed for that they didn't receive or see come to pass. There are many things we have prayed for that haven't happened yet. Take notice that I said, "haven't happened yet." That means that it will happen, but it

just hasn't manifested in our life yet. There are some dead things, dry things, dead dreams, and dead visions that we have forgotten because we have gotten tired of waiting. Today, I am here to say that heaven is voice-activated and you can speak to the dead things. Speak to your business, marriage, health, vision, and dreams and speak life. As in Ezekiel 37, there were some dried-up bones that needed to have a wind blow in order for them to live. It can live again, we just need wind from the Most High, and we need to prophesy again over what is dead. In order for dead things to live again, they must have breath and they must have life. The word of God that is spoken by us brings forth life. Problems and situations will arise, but we have the authority to speak the word over them. What is dry can be watered with the word through our voice. When we speak it is activated into the atmosphere to awaken and speak life. Just like in the beginning, God said "Let there be." We must speak accordingly as it was because the same power lives within us. Today, whatever is dry in your life, begin to speak to it. Until you water it and speak life into it, it will stay dead. What seems like it had to happen can be shifted with your voice. It may have happened, but it is temporary and it can live again.

We are going to experience the wilderness at times, but we can also get through our wilderness by speaking and activating heaven over our situation. We sometimes stay stuck longer and in the wilderness because we rehearse the problem and not the promise. Again, we must rehearse what God says and not what the world said, the doctor said, and your friend said. God's word is final and true. God isn't guessing when he provides us a word from heaven, He knows the truth.

Imagine you are walking on acres of farmland. It is your farm and it hasn't rained in weeks. The crops are starting to look dingy and dry of course. Are you going to mumble and complain? You may for a little while but you are going to try and come up with a plan to make your crops to live again. Speak to the atmosphere that rain shall come forth over your crops and they shall live again. At the right set time, the rain will come forth. We have to speak to what is dry so water can provide life again. Your situation may seem dim and it may seem to not be moving. Today, activate your faith in God, begin to speak life over your situation again and watch God move. We can't stand still having a pity party and allow death to take over. We are overcomers by the blood and we have the authority to speak life

DRY BONES

because of He who provides life. For every negative thing, there is a positive that can be taken from it. We must know how to activate the positive and change our perspective. We have to speak life again and believe in who He is. Decree today that what was dry will live and thrive now.

"Behold, I was brought forth in iniquity, and in sin my mother conceived me"

PSALM 51:5

Damaged Goods

It is normal to believe and perceive what will occur by what we see in the natural. Sometimes what we see may not be ideal for what we want to occur. Our normal view also has to include a supernatural view and perspective. We are the first spiritual beings created to live on Earth. When we dwell only on what we see, we limit God who is a protocol breaker. If He is a God of the impossible, then that means we need to expect the best to occur. There is nothing at all normal about the way God operates. This is why it is so hard to trace and understand spiritual things without a spiritual mindset. We need to divorce the limiting beliefs that limit our Father's wonders over our life. He wants us to shift our mind to operate without limits.

Before the beginning of time, many of us have felt some type of rejection, offense or even abandonment by someone we love. This is because trauma or rejection has disturbed our normal life. Something came and violated our feelings and made us feel below our creator's standards for our life. The feeling of rejection can bring about stagnation, low self-esteem, a muted voice, depression, and other feelings that don't allow us to operate in our truth. When we begin to carry what was said about us, done to us, or how others made us feel, it is detrimental to our future. We begin to deal with the hurt by crying or just becoming numb to what happened to us. The pain that we carry can carry on into our adult lives and cause even greater harm. When we carry the stigma of rejection, we attract other hurt people into our lives. We also get more of the same treatment because hurt people hurt others. The only true antidote for the rejection is to seek deliverance and help from the Father. We have to begin to understand who we are, and why we were created. We can't allow anyone who didn't design our lives to define our lives. This causes us to certainly live below our values. If the pain is not dealt with, then it flows to our offspring and operates in our relationships as well.

Though many things may have happened to us, it is not what defines us or makes us. Oftentimes, we learn to live with the pain and survive, but not heal from the pain inside. It is so important to deal with what injures and hurts us inside. The pain can bring about sickness, anxiety, and fear and cause us to stagnate ourselves in life. The thing about rejection is that oftentimes we carry it not knowing it is within us. We move in our lives holding on to the spirit and not breaking the stronghold. It is our portion to walk in freedom, healing and our full truth. We have to deal with our issues and understand that rejection is not our portion, but healing is. We have a master surgeon that wants to operate on us.

We all have been to the grocery store and come across items that have been damaged. Oftentimes, they are thrown away or marked down on clearance. We live in the world and we are just like those damaged goods. We have encountered life and sin and it causes us to carry damage. We may also carry sins of our generation that we did not commit. The good thing is that we have an advocate in heaven that wants us to be fully restored and live a life of wholeness. The Father has made us in His image. We have a book in heaven that shows who we are and what we are on Earth to fulfill. The father already knows our day-to-day and the future. We however have to live the journey and receive the revelation of our book in heaven. The value we hold is not lost because we have damage and dirt thrown on us. We are seen in our father's eyes as a masterpiece. We can be restored from any damage and made whole. What happens in our life does not change our worth. Our Father always sees us on purpose, and not as damaged.

During our trying times and in our damaged place is when our character is built and we gain wisdom and truth. The damage is what allows us to know who God is within us. It allows us to seek Him and fully understand our father's role in our lives. Without damage and dirt, we wouldn't need our Father. Our value comes from within and not outside. Our Father is able to take us in our current state and make us new. The damage is used for your testimony to bring glory to the Father. Don't despise the injury because it is temporary. The bruising will be used to place you back together again. When our father refines us, He makes us better and stronger. He brings the qualities that already exist in us and allows us to operate in them fully. The damage caused us to place a mask over ourselves. God comes along and allows us to remove the mask and operate from wholeness. Although we have areas that may have received damage, we are still valuable and able to be used fully by God. Our damage is there to make us greater to grow us and show us who we are fully in God. Character is built during the storm and so is patience. Your circumstance and anything that may limit you does not create your value. God creates and adds value to you.

PHASE II
Chasing Eden

> *"Behold, the days come, saith the Lord, that I will establish a new covenant with the house of Israel and with the house of Judah"*
>
> JEREMIAH 31-34

Kingdom

But seek first his kingdom and his righteousness, and all these things will be given to you as well.

MATTHEW 6:33

Do you know who God has ordained and called you to be before the beginning of time? There are books in the heavens with your name on them that specify your specific gifts and destiny that were ordained before you were born. We should be coming into agreement with our book of destiny. God wants us to partake and move in our full destiny. Our father gives us pieces of the bigger puzzle through prophecy, dreams, and speaking to us regarding our future. We can only find out mysteries and obtain information when we are walking with Him and seeking him. When we seek Him, then we can begin to see His hand and His glory. The glory is where the infinite beauty of God manifests and causes wonders on Earth. It is in His glory that we see healings, visions, miracles, wonders, angelic encounters, power, dead come to life, darkness come to light, transformations, honor, riches, and deliverance. This is the Kabod which means His weight. We must know that even in times of trial, God is faithful. When we look at the world, it seems to be going in a direction that is evil and may be scary at times. We are not to rely on the Earthly systems for our life. We must look to the Kingdom and the heavenly perspective. We have treasures that are laid up for us in heaven. In the treasure room, everything that was stolen from you has your name on it. The treasures are hidden just for us and belong to us. We are His chosen that are anointed for a purpose to be fulfilled on Earth. In addition, He is our guide, truth, and provides the promise to us and we must trust Him. He is the God that gives the promise and keeps the promise if we walk in obedience and faith. The faithfulness of God is our hope and trust in our life. The resurrection power of God trumps any attack of the enemy against us. We have to remember we serve a God who nothing can stand against, and who has armies of angels to fight for us and with us. The days ahead for you shall be blessed if you stay focused and anchored. For those who remain faithful and steadfast in faith, the physical manifestations of His glory and promise shall prevail. His treasures will come forth and be revealed to those who walk in His ways. Today, begin to receive the treasures in your hand by faith.

Many of us have been misled to walk in religion, tradition, and denominations and not knowing or establishing a relationship with God. We are called to be ambassadors of the Kingdom of God and we are Kingdom citizens. As a citizen, you have full access and benefits to everything that your father owns. We are called to walk by kingdom principles with authority and power. Your title doesn't matter when you are saved and a citizen. What matters is your obedience and your surrender to accept the Father as Lord of your life. Jesus Christ came to Earth to establish Kingdom and break sin. The Kingdom is governed by the King of Kings and we have access to the keys of the kingdom. We also have an advocate that is there to help us move forward in life, the Holy Spirit. When we are saved, that is one step, but we are to begin to live with a renewed mind and a new lifestyle. We are to change our thoughts with the word to think from above. When we walk in Kingdom, the rules of the Earth can be bypassed because Kingdom breaks protocol and has advantage. In the Kingdom, there are miracles, health, wealth, righteousness, promotion, joy, peace, angels, helpers, etc and all good things. Even before you were born, your name was announced and written with a daily recording of your existence. It is for us to access our records in heaven by prayer, fasting, and seeking the Father with our whole heart. There is a purpose assigned and ordained by God for us to fulfill on Earth. There are those assigned to us that we are called to touch. "We are an answer for someone, and someone is an answer for us." We can't walk in fulfillment in our life without knowing our true worth and identity. When we don't know our true worth, we will downgrade ourselves and live below our true value.

We are born with a voice that activates heaven to Earth. We have the authority to establish things on Earth according to heaven's will for our lives. We have an inheritance that has already been written and promised to us by our father. If we stay rooted and grounded, we will see the fullness of our promise come forth to Earth. Each of us is called to a mountain of influence on the Earth. Those mountains are business, family, education, religion, Media and Communications, government, & Entertainment. We are each called to influence one or more of these mountains to empower and bring heaven to Earth. We must know what is detailed in our book and who we are called to be. It starts with seeking God and letting Him provide insight and knowledge to us. You are born as a winner and victory is certainly your birthright. It is time that we walk by the standards of the Kingdom and not below God's standard for our lives. We are called to be powerful, wealthy, and advancers of the Kingdom. As I write this book, I realize that God is taking me through a journey of deliverance to remove things from my family line that was damaged. He has called many of us to be curse breakers for our family. One term I remember is when he told me I was called to be a repairer of the breach for my family. I understood it slightly, but I had to research the meaning of it more. When something is breached, it means that something was broken and failed because of a violation of a law. In the Bible, it speaks about being called to repair and fix what is broken in the generations and bring it back into right standing not only for ourselves but for others as well. (Isaiah 58:12) In order for us to walk in the fullness of the inheritance, we must first break covenants with the attachments from our family line where the laws were broken. This is a must because this allows the enemy to have an open door to delay, stagnate, and keep us away from what is ours. It is time for us to break covenants with any evil covenant established in our lineage so our legacy can move forth. We have access to the courts of heaven where Jesus is our just judge and advocate, and we can speak our case to cancel accusations of the enemy that was placed in heaven against us and our family. Just like there is a book of destiny, there is a book of written accusations that need to be cancelled. We must cancel the covenants and linkage to the enemy that has our family's name on it and our name so we can walk in freedom. Our Father wants us to walk in our full inheritance.

Tithing

We are aware that money and wisdom are important in our lives. God doesn't want us to be poor but to be wealthy and good stewards of what is ours. Money itself is not evil, but greed and allowing money to control us is. When we make a decision that alters our position in the Kingdom because of money, that is evil. We should certainly desire to have wealth. The Kingdom is wealthy. We must not just hold wealth in our hands but in our minds, and thoughts and be sowers of the word and money. We need increase to proceed in doing what we are called to do. The world might have you think that having a 9-5 is what we are supposed to do for the rest of our lives. Also, we can't be wealthy if we are not in entertainment or an athlete. Don't get me wrong; those things are great, but we must seek God to see what we are called to do. The father wants to provide us with inventions and ideas, to help produce wealth in our lives. We must destroy the idea of poverty, and just enough; we are called to walk in more than enough. As influencers on the Earth, we are to walk in the mountains we are called to empower so wealth can be released. The Father is the one that provides us with the ability to obtain wealth when we take action and move and speak in obedience to His will. Heaven has an endless supply that is for us. There is no famine, recession, or lack in heaven. If we are citizens of heaven, there should be no lack in our lives. When we learn to sow the right way and give in generosity, our seeds produce a bountiful harvest.

Our minds must be expanded to think thoughts from above because heaven is about expansion and increase. The wealth that we obtain is not just for us, but it is to expand the Kingdom. He wants others to know His goodness and His ways through His children. When we see Kingdom miracles, it is so we can know His goodness and His truth. It is so wonderful when someone starts from nothing, and we see them built up by God to become millionaires in life. This is when we know our God is real and wellable. All we can say is " But God!" He did it not man, but He did it. He is also the supplier of our business and our great supply comes from Him. It is time for us to expand our knowledge to accept the kingdom principles of wealth. I am not asking for my house note to be paid, but I want a debt-free home that is marvelous and grand. My God can do it because I have seen Him do it for others. He wants us to ask big, think big, and walk in faith for big.

The tithe is more about obedience to God. It is not about a certain percentage. Under the new covenant, it says for us to give generously from the heart. The first tithe was made by Abram in Genesis 14:20 and Abram gave a tenth of everything. During this time, everything was people, cattle, and food. The Levitical tithe or sacred tithe was given to the Levites and Priest. This tithe was used to help those less fortunate and in times of famine. The tithe was done either two to three times a year only. (Depends on the Year) Tithes were a requirement of those that owned land and crops. Many have created a falsehood of tithes and walk by man's rules. We must first understand the economic system of giving and receiving in the Kingdom. It is very important to give to the poor and those in need around us not just to the church. My husband has a non-profit Empac Nation where he gives to the poor and to his sports program. There are many kids that can't afford the program nor shoes or essentials to play the sport. We don't turn them away, but God helps us to provide for them. We need to give to organizations, people and those in need that demonstrate kingdom ways. We have to watch where we place our money because we make a covenant agreement with the receiver as we give.

For many years, my mother gave the same amount weekly to the church, and on occasion, offerings to help with the fair and building funds. I had no idea how giving worked, but I knew it was good. I was well aware that poverty was satanic because why would a good God allow poverty. We read about a God that helps others and lacked nothing. The key to unlocking wealth we can agree is in our release. What we give out, it is a law that it will return to us multiplied. We can't go wrong with our giving. We should always be ready to give time, and seeds, and sow into those in need. The tithe to church is not the only place where we should tithe. God says that when we see someone in need, we are to provide help as he leads us. It is also an important principle to know where to give. We should seek the Father where to place our money at. When we sow a seed, we are sowing into that person's word and house. When we sow, it should be a place that is just not receiving but also giving back. We should not place our money and make a covenant with the wrong house or people. This is why we hear the term good ground. God will give us the amount to give, where to give, and when to give. No one should be telling us an amount that God said to give; this is misleading and manipulation, not God. When we listen to God, we are not bamboozled by man and greed. God will provide more

TITHING

than enough seed for those that give diligently. We are called to fund the Kingdom projects as led by God. We must always be led in our giving because our giving creates a covenant with that party. When we walk by his obedience, we can be sure that our money will not be withheld but be multiplied and increased. We must also know scripture and activate our voice over our seeds. Name your seeds and declare that they shall be multiplied back to you.

Birthing

All of us entered this Earth through a process of birthing through our mother's womb. The birthing process is a process that takes months for us to grow and fully develop into a young infant. Just like in the physical, we also have a birthing process at every level in the spiritual realm. We go through testing and pains, and gain insight during our birthing in the spirit. During this birthing process, much pressure is applied and we are often pushed out of our comfort zone. We can't grow and transform while still in our comfort zone. The growth and stretching happen when we move in obedience. It is certainly a time when our Father stretches us to new things and prepares us for the next season of our life. The pressure that is applied is where creativity comes from. This is where we are launched into a new place to go to the next destination written in your journey.

It is now time for us to receive the manifestations of heaven and see them on Earth. The heavenly blessing does not come how we think or when we think necessary. God will use others to bless us and also to help thrust us to the next level. The more we access God and seek Him, the more of His

BIRTHING

glory and mysteries we learn. His glory is an atmosphere of Eden where everything must bow to Him and we see wonders. He wants us to be in this atmosphere and reside there forever. We must also begin to think and ponder on things above and not worldly things. We must always have a kingdom perspective when we are birthing. It is by our faith and obedience that the blessings begin to flow in our life. Just like with a baby's birth, in the spirit, we get tired and grow weary. We can walk in confidence knowing that the Father is our strength and sends us increased power during our walk. We have to truly seek Him at all parts of our process. The manifestation is proof of who the Father is, and what He can do and will do in us. We must activate our voice to speak what heaven is saying about our situation and our life. The Holy Spirit is an important advocate in our lives and reveals the truth.

We must rehearse the things that belong to us so they can be written over our hearts and our minds. In our lives living wells of Christ, we must activate the wells in our lives. Many things lie dormant if we don't activate them and birth them forth.

Today, trust the next chapter of your life. The author of your life has not changed nor changed His mind. He has a perfect track record, and He is faithful. God is ready to turn the pages of your book and blow His Ruach. The Ruach is His mighty wind, spirit and breath and when the pages blow, He is accelerating you into the next level where you belong. Everything that is out of alignment is blown into its right place. He is the God of promise, and He is the promise keeper. As He blows His wind, everything begins to align with His purpose for your life. You will stay the course and have a full successful birth of your destiny. The birthing process has made you stronger and more of a danger to the enemy. It is now a time for the due season. Even when people and things come against you, God is still there. You shall not miss your time. God's word is true and final, and He is not like man that He can lie; He will not lie. You shall not miss or miscarry what belongs to you. Get in agreement with His plans and will for your life. You are carrying the gifts and the blessings for you and others. Remember the blessing already has your name on it, and it is time for the manifestation from heaven to Earth. Your quest and journey into Eden shall be fulfilled as you go higher and deeper in Him. Don't settle for less when He has many things of great value and worth just for you. The journey is written with your name and the destiny belongs to you and it is packed with blessings on top of blessings. You are valuable to Him, and your destiny is value-packed and worth the journey. We must be careful to birth with care and secure our blessings and gift at every level and stage. We are glory carriers of what He has placed within us, and no one else can provide spiritual blessings but the Father.

"When You Feel Stuck You Are Housing The Answer That Is Waiting To Be Revealed & Released!"

> *"And in your offspring shall all the nations of the Earth be blessed because you have obeyed my voice"*
>
> GENESIS 22:18

The Torch

How many times have we heard that the grave is the most wealthy place on Earth. This is because many torches have died, and they have not been picked up. Nothing in your family line is lost, but it must be picked up and carried forth with knowledge. We are called to carry a torch for our family legacy as kingdom children. The torch that we carry must break any curse that is operating in our family line. The Father has called our families to experience generational blessings and favor and not curses. Our Father did not intend for us to carry rejection, trauma, sickness, pain, depression, low self-esteem, and other strongholds that are not our portion. We are also not called to walk in delay, procrastination, worry, defeat, or any limitation that tries to attempt to deter our purpose. The great news is that we also have the Holy Spirit as our helper, tutor, teacher, guide, and corrector to guide us through our life. Under the new covenant where Jesus Christ is eternal High Priest in heaven, we have a full inheritance covenant and it can't be broken. The covenant allows us to experience wealth, salvation, freedom, joy, peace, new birth, protection and every attribute afforded to us in heaven. It all belongs to us as children of God. That is great news! Just like our parents, our spiritual Father wants

THE TORCH

to leave us an inheritance that adds to our life. Our heavenly Father wants us to live with an inheritance package now on Earth. We are to live heaven out on Earth. When we live heaven on Earth, it benefits us, our legacy and brings others to Christ. Then we can live an even greater life when we enter the after-life. We are seated in heavenly places and our prayers are heard down to Earth. We must activate daily and surrender daily to the Father. What belongs to us has to be brought down and manifested on Earth. Through a growing relationship, we are able to activate revelation and receive downloads from heaven. As we take the steps to move with our torch, we are filled and fueled to elevate and move higher in the purpose and promise. You are called to be the called out one for your family. Your family legacy depends on you now, and your children as well. The torch you carry has assignments also attached to it. We have certain people that are assigned just to us. They are depending on us to move so they can move forward. It's time to take the torch and be relentless in your walk. The promise doesn't come easy but the Holy Spirit helps to order our steps and it is necessary. The father is the way, the truth, and the light. We are called to carry our torch and light up this Earthly realm. We sometimes fall short, but God is still with us and will see us through. God is always our answer and Exodus. Our torch can't run out as long as we live on Earth. We are called to walk on purpose and help others to do the same. Today, know that you are powerful, strong, and equipped and it is time to carry your torch.

My father transitioned to heaven when I was only eight years old. I did not think of the gifts or the purpose that was within me. The process was very hard and it took a big toll on my grades, and I also felt lots of rejection and hurt during that time. I realized later in life that there were things that I needed to do in my family that were left undone. His torch had burnt out, but it was time for mine to shine. When I look back, I am fully aware that I have overcome many obstacles that were meant to take me out. I am thankful, grateful, and blessed that I know God. It is a part of my torch to write this book today and continue to speak as a voice for God. Yes, it gets hard, but when we look at our promise, we know it belongs to us. It is not just for us and our family but also for others. I don't know about you, but I want to see how the promise looks. I want to receive and walk in all that God has for me. We owe it to ourselves and our legacy depends on it. As I write, I think about not only my legacy walking in generational blessings but having a written blueprint for kingdom instruction through my writing. It is time to grow; move with your torch so one day it will be passed on. We must be aware that many depend on our torch and it must not burn out. Remember your destiny is sealed and belongs to you. Everything that God has for you is backed in heaven, and God will keep you so nothing can harm you for you are his representation on Earth.

"The Spirit Is Our Flame that never burns but tutors us to our truth!"

I Prophesy Now

I prophesy now a sudden mighty wind over your business, family, marriage, and your womb. I call back the aborted dreams and ideas that died within and speak life and blessing over them. I command the aborted dreams to live, thrive and come back to life now. I prophesy agreement with the divine intentions of heaven over your life today. I call forth the mind and memory of heaven. I prophesy that your days ahead are blessed, your mind is blessed, your name is blessed and your identity is anchored in God. Let there be everlasting streams of income, increase, and agreement with heaven. We cancel and rebuke delay, worry, procrastination,

THE TORCH

and every limitation is broken by the fiery axe of the Spirit now. I decree that marriages shall begin to align and resemble heaven's will. I prophesy wealth, health, strength, and divine acceleration over your life. May the daily bread of heaven be your portion daily. I prophesy that your eyes are opened to what heaven says, and your ears hear the Father now. I prophesy that you are seated in the promise. The book of Purpose and Destiny is now received. God remembers you and all that you have done. I prophesy that the perfect promise of heaven that belongs to you shall come forth, IN Jesus' Name!

"How You Started, Is Not How You Finish Because Your Destiny Is Written & Sealed!"

"Let the favor of the Lord our God be upon us, and establish the work of our hands upon us; yes, establish the work of our hands!"

PSALM 90:17

Favor

Favor is a popular topic that we always speak about as followers of Christ. When we accept Christ, we accept the new covenant which is binding and eternal. This means that the covenant Jesus made on the cross can never be broken and when we agree to salvation, we have full benefits. Now, there are some things that we have to follow under the Covenant and we have to receive the Holy Spirit as well. For example, in the word, it says that a man that finds a wife has found favor. That means that when a husband finds his rib and treats her right, he has God's favor. Favor can go before us because of our relationship with the Father and allow us to see doors open, protocols broken, rules broken, and things established that would not be ordinarily. When we follow God and have relationship, we are backed and represented by heaven, so God can use anyone to bless us. Your direct connection to the father places us in a position of royalty where we have the advantage to connect with the right people to place us in the right places and bring forth divine opportunities.

Favor is something added or extra to what is due to you. You have special treatment and you walk in the finer things because of who you are. As we receive favor, we receive something we can't obtain by ourselves. He wants us to access and use our authority in life to position us to receive favor and wear favor. The father wants us to experience favor and walk in favor daily. Favor shows how much the Father loves us and wants to provide for us. He wants us to have access to the things that belong to us, and we are to have advantage over the world. We are VIPs in the heavenly realm, and the Father has also given us authority and dominion on Earth through His Kingdom. The Kingdom works supersede the natural realm when we use the power and authority given to us by the Father. Our Father's word says that "the wealth of the wicked shall be laid up for the just." (Proverbs 13:22) This is a word of favor that our Father will allow the wicked to bless His children. The word also says that "the last shall be first and the first shall be last." (Matthew 20:16) When we have favor, we begin to see wonders, overflow, and abundance and the streams of God begin to flow in our lives. The things that the Father shows us sometimes seem unorthodox. This is when the Lord wants us to line up our faith with His word and believe. We can't look at what we see, but we must focus on God's promise and favor to produce the promise. We have to have a heavenly perspective when we walk in favor. The things we go through and the circumstances don't change our value or God's plan. God is a protocol breaker and He always has a ram in the bush to turn around what is not our portion in life. I recall the words of Apostle Martin always saying to us "One word, one touch, one moment in his presence can change your current position." You are not meant to stay in the pit or the wilderness, you are meant to see heaven on Earth. God is a now God and doesn't need time. Yes, He is a God of goodness, mercy, grace and also justice. He will protect His children and He gives us His word to combat the enemy and do warfare.

FAVOR

Today, I trust God. I believe in the wonders and miracles of God. I know that our Father has given us the same power and authority to bring forth blessings over our life. We must; however, follow the kingdom principles and put on our armor. He wants the best for His children and our legacy. Favor will allow the activation of more than enough, and allow those to bless you and provide lavish things. Favor will open doors to great opportunities you are not qualified for. Favor will provide what money can't buy. We must know that our Father provides us with favor, divine relationships, associations, and favor is our portion. Today, I declare crazy favor, increase, abundance, and rainbows of favor come forth perfectly. Favor locate those reading this message now. In Jesus' Name.

"I have set my rainbow in the clouds, and it will be a sign of the covenant between me and the Earth"

GENESIS 9:13-16

Rainbows Coming Now

Yes indeed, it won't be long now, God's Decree. "Things are going to happen fast your head will swim, one thing on the heels of the other. You won't be able to keep up. Everything will happen at once, and everywhere you look, blessings! "(Amos 9:13-15)

The rainbow was a sign of God's covenant from the time of creation that He is establishing a covenant with His children. God's covenant is sealed with the blood and can't be broken. The rainbow has seven colors and layers which represent the completion of God's work. He is the beginning and the end which means His word is finished and done. When I see a rainbow, I begin to think about the promises He has made to me. I know that His word is true and He will protect and back His promise to us. It is now time for the layers of the blessings of His covenant to unfold and be released in our life. Each layer represents a different level of blessing and each color has a meaning ordained for a purpose. He knew our name before the beginning of our existence in the womb. It was written day by day in the heavens. This means that our name has been established with a God-ordained purpose and destiny. It has been hidden from us until it is time for us to unwrap one of the promises in our life. The rainbows of blessing stand in the heavens waiting to be unwrapped and manifested in our life. Now is the time for activation of the promises. Not just one promise that belongs to us but many promises. Today, I stand on the word of Amos 9 that we are about to receive blessings and layers of rainbows come into our lives quickly. It is a new season of wonders, acceleration and the divine suddenlies from God. What was held up, delayed and sabotaged shall be released now upon our lives. Victory is our birthright, and our Father has won. (It is done)

I had a vivid dream of destiny a while back. In the dream, I was looking at a long sheet of paper with numbers of all sizes large, small and medium-sized numbers. I began to add the numbers of the dream but it went on a long way. I could remember some of the numbers, but it was a lengthy list. God said to me before the dream ended; this is your case in heaven of recompense. This is what has been held up and lost through your family line and belongs to you. This case is double for your trouble what has been held up from suffering loss and damages that are owed. I just began to thank God for the release of my case from heaven to Earth. Now, of course, the enemy knows about the case as well; so I began to go through some warfare as well. God started giving me the strategy of things that needed to be broken. I began to read scripture over my case and rehearse God's word. I was also led to fast during this time. The Lord says that when the enemy comes like a flood, He will uphold a standard against the enemy on our behalf. (Isaiah 59:19) I declare today, that we shall recover all, and we shall break the covenants made through our ancestral line made with the enemy. God is a God of justice, recompense, and manifestation as well and nothing can stand against God. His mighty hand will bring forth and protect our promise. We also have to utilize our angels assigned to us and command them to work on our behalf. It is time to believe again, and trust that every blessing that is ours shall come forth now.

Today, I prophesy that the rainbow of God is released now. I received a land inheritance from my family line. Now, this was a great blessing, but there was also much bondage upon my family line that had to be broken from our lineage. This land has been in our family for hundreds of years, but there was a breach made through many of my ancestors with the enemy that opened evil altars as well. Land is a great investment certainly. The evil altars that were established knowingly or unknowingly have caused delay, stagnation, and many things to deter our inheritance as a family. This is why we must watch who we make covenants with. Covenants can be made through societies, witchcraft, fornication, and many other ways that attach evil and open doors. I am glad that God has chosen and trusted me to be the repairer of the breach.

I had another dream of destiny regarding my family line. In this dream, I was in a fine restaurant talking to well-known stars and others I don't know. I was seated on a bench waiting to be seated at the table. I did recognize one person that was eating before we went to the table. God was saying that this is a sign that we are not patient and accept less than what belongs to us. Then we were seated at the table with others. I recognized one of my cousins sitting next to me. There was a chalice cup that spilled in front of me with a deep purple liquid. I started to clean the liquid and the rest disintegrated. Then there were appetizers were served. I could see a beautiful fruit tray made in the shape of a capital P. I passed the fruit down to my cousin next to me. God said that I was the repairer of the breach that would begin to break poverty off of the family line and it would be passed down the lineage. This was such a powerful dream, yet there was also a great deal of fasting and breaking off of covenants as well. I realized that God was showing me a piece of the promise, but He also had to show me what was holding back the promise. This road has not been easy by far, but I know it is necessary for me and those attached to me. I'm looking forward to my promise that I know is mine and shall come forth.

Success

There is no one definition to what success is. We have different views and viewpoints on success. There is also not just one method to achieve success. There is, however, an ultimate plan that is written with your name in heaven for your daily life. This plan will bring optimal results because it is made by the manufacturer. That plan is God's plan and purpose for your life. No one can walk in that exact plan but you. You do have the choice to reject the plan and move with your own plan. You are also gifted and equipped and ready for the plan in heaven. You were born with gifts and blessings that belong to you. We are limited to our success when we go our route. We may see success with money, but will we have the wisdom, peace and all the attributes of heaven within. Our plan can never be as good as God's plan because His thoughts are higher than ours. We also have a teacher and guide in the Holy Spirit.

The Bible tells us that those who wait on the Lord will prosper and see His goodness. I am a true believer that as I walk in obedience and according to His plan, I will see my full promise come forth. I want all the things that belong to me. We do have to remain rooted and grounded. We must also be aware that our success also is for others. We are called to walk on purpose for ourselves and others. No matter what success means to you, we must seek God first. True fulfillment comes from above and not man. Only with Him can we see and experience true greatness and fulfillment. Our lives should reflect Him and His goodness. God is my true source and He provides for us through resources and open doors. Always look above for your help comes from God, and many are waiting on you so they can walk in purpose. Destiny and divine success are what God has for all of us. Today, look above because it is time to access Eden and live in the land where we receive heaven on Earth. Remember that you are what God says, and you can have all that God says. It's time for us to walk in Eden and the supernatural atmosphere so we can receive heavenly things on Earth. It is through our voice, the keys, and our obedience that we will obtain Eden. Be relentless in your walk with God because Eden awaits and all the treasures of heaven with your name on it.

"Your Success Comes Through Process, Growth, Revelation, and Obedience!"

"The one who call you is faithful, and he will do it"

1 THESSALONIANS 5:24

The Promise

When I look over my life, I am grateful and very thankful. There was a time when I felt stagnant, lost, and alone for sure. I am thankful that this is when God began to reveal to me who I was within Him. He began to download Kingdom principles and the foundations of Kingdom within me. Growing up Catholic, I knew God, but of course, there were too many rules and traditions that were taught which did not bring true revelation to me. God doesn't want us to care what the world thinks of us, but know we are His chosen and loved by Him. He is the only one who can validate who we are. I am thankful that as I began to write and know purpose, he also sent healing and deliverance. I now anchor my identity in God and Him alone. This is my fourth book that is ordained by God's plan. I am fully aware that there are many things He has called me to do. One step and one day at a time. I continue to write, prepare, teach, and transform daily. We need to be transformed because this allows us to be taught and changed within. Now, this life is not easy for sure. I am not without fault nor perfect, but certainly, I serve a perfect God. He upholds me and guides my steps in this life. This promise and your promise are big because it impacts more than just you. We have assignments we are

THE PROMISE

charged with, and someone is assigned to you as well. The promise is linked to many so it is important, vital and significant to your plan.

I have a childhood friend that has a daughter that suffered from Lupus. We call her Kay for short. From age 11, she battled with the disease, and her life was changed forever. One thing that Kay did through her trials is that she loved, inspired and fought hard. She started an organization to help others battling Lupus fight and be a support system. This was so awesome to me because her assignment was to help others to get through while she was also going through. She journaled and wrote many details of her life while battling her illness. She asked her mom to make sure she published her journey to help others. Kay's Kidneys failed and she passed away at the ripe age of 24. I was blessed to meet one of the young ladies she inspired. The young lady was inspired by Kay and wanted to meet Kay's mother. She & Kay had set up to meet the week after her death. She was looking forward to the meeting and was devastated to hear Kay had passed. This so touched my heart to see the impact Kay had on so many people. If Kay pushed to touch lives while she was sick, what's holding you up? We have to move forward for God, ourself, those assigned to us, our families and Kay as well. Remember Kay in times when it gets hard because her story is so awesome. May God bless all those battling Lupus and spring forth healing and restoration. You can also read about Kay's story @ doitforkay.com.

We often say we are waiting on God to do it. Today, God is saying that the promise already exists and is ready. He's waiting on us to get started and move from him and with him. The promise is already in our belly and we are fully equipped to win. You may feel stuck because you have failed to activate purpose for your life. We will feel stuck when we fail to listen, hear and activate promises. Now, of course, the enemy comes to try and steal, deter and take us off course. We have to remember that the promise and the promise keeper are greater than the enemy. We also have angels in heaven assigned to us to help us. Your promise and heaven are voice-activated first. We must move forward by rehearsing what God says and moving in obedience and wisdom. He said He shall supply all of our needs. We get stuck in the how, when and how long of things. I am reminded of how unorthodox our father is. He doesn't think like man, lie, nor can anything obstruct his hand. What hinders us or stumps us has already been answered and is known by God. This is why we have to walk forward and remove the limitations and the box.

Our promise requires us to move forward in revelation and by faith in what God shows us and tells us. We can't be moved by what we see. Now that is certainly not always easy being that it is right in your face. We have to be diligent in protecting our promise. Our promise is so big and many depend on what occurs in our life. This is why we must guard our hearts, ears, eyes, and our words as well. We have power in our hands and in our mouth as well. You wear the authority of God to speak forth and move forth in your promise. God will send the help, the word, and the instruction to us. We must do our part too fast, pray, align, agree, speak, and move in obedience. Your promise requires stretching, preparation and trust for sure. I was speaking to a great friend and prayer partner, and we both have had some intense warfare but yet encouraged. God spoke and said regardless of the warfare, Am I not God that can move regardless of what's happening in the natural. I am the Jehovah Gibbor that fights for my children. That is confirmation that God is certainly overturning the assignments of the enemy and you are represented by heaven! Praise God!

THE PROMISE

Today, be relentless to follow the promise and the plan. This is the ultimate plan that man can't manufacture. Don't hold back who you are because others don't accept you. Don't allow the enemy to steal your shine, your flow, and your glow. We certainly have to hear God and know our true identity. If we don't know Him, we will second guess the manufacturer. The power, the gift, and the spirit live in you. The gift giver created the gifts within. God is the genius who made you perfect. Don't doubt the creator. It's your time to win and walk in Eden. It is not easy by any means, and the warfare gets intense at times. It is necessary and rewarding because you are someone's answer. The promise is revealed and hidden for you to access. We must partner and seek the father for the answer. We don't wake up just knowing our true purpose. We have to seek the answers through prayer and relationship. Also, ask; we must knock on His door and ask Him. I am believing in the promise and the rainbows that are manifesting. I trust Daddy, and I know Daddy loves me. I strive today to walk in Eden. This is an atmosphere of greatness where the impossible is made possible. The atmosphere where the spirit transcends what we see naturally with our eyes. It is unorthodox, sure, and unexplainable to many. It's time for the fulfillment of your promise because you are exactly what and who God says! You are Significant, Special, and Worthy!

"Your promise is not meant to die or be buried, but it is meant to live, Be Seen, & Manifest Fully!

Prayer of Recovery

In Jesus' Name, I command all unbroken curses of the ancestral line operating in my life be broken. I unbind myself from any linkage to the ancestral lines of evil and break the bounds now. I declare that virtue and goodness are brought back to me and my lineage now. I declare that every delay, limitation, and attempt of the enemy to bring discord is cancelled and annulled from my life. Now, every evil spirit and attachment must bow to the name of Jesus and the blood. Every evil covenant, we break and denounce and consume with the Holy Spirit consuming fires. We lose and destroy the fires of heaven over every satanic limitation and linkage now. We cancel every word curse, financial blocker, and inheritance blocker now. We break off temporary shortages and just enough over our life.

Now we decree an abundance of rivers over our life. Every need is met and we receive great success in our finances, business, marriages and children. I decree what was lost is brought back alive by the fire of the Holy Spirit now. I decree the full inheritance of the land, the money, the favor and all that belongs to me is my portion and comes forth now. From this day, I decree success and the divine destiny that belongs to me manifest now.

(Review what is attaching itself in patterns to your family line, look for prayers to break these things)

I Am Wealthy, Wealth Is My Portion Today!

Wisdom, Wealth, Health & Joy belongs to me!

Lord, we thank You that the profit of the Earth is for me, I now take hold and come into agreement with your perfect will for me. Wealth and Financial Increase is my portion, now! I come into agreement with my book of destiny and receive all blessings from my book now.

THE PROMISE

My Portion

Success is my portion

Wealth Is my portion

Wisdom is my portion

Insight is my portion

Knowledge is my portion

Favor is my portion

Sound mind is my portion

Understanding of mysteries is mine

A blessed legacy is mine

A blessed marriage ordained by God is my portion

Riches is my portion

The treasures of heaven is my portion.

Prayers

Lord, You are the supplier of every need, and thank You that You go forth to rebuke the devourer on my behalf.

Lord thanks, my finances are released from all satanic influences, and from any contaminated soil and it is now free to produce a bountiful harvest.

Lord, I dismantle every evil agent that is trying to steal my money, I break poverty from my life. I decree that this day, increase is mine and my money shall flow with rivers of abundance and I receive financial wealth now.

I break generational poverty over my life and my generational line. I now receive the Economies of Kingdom Wealth and Kingdom Prosperity. Amen

"If you don't know your true identity and worth, you will downgrade who you are and live below God's standards for your life."

~ PROPHET TIFFANY EALY

Who Am I

Daughter, Son, Chosen, Backed by Heaven, Righteous, Talented, Gifted, Loved, Unique, Beautiful, Wonderfully Made, Powerful, Voice, Conduit, Ambassador, Citizen of Kingdom, Worthy, Valuable, More Than Enough, King, Queen, Amazing, Incredible, Important, Anointed, Called-Out, Faithful, Obedient, Giving, Masterpiece, Irreplaceable, Treasured, Creative, Kind, Honest, Forgiving, Whole, Restored, Healthy, Free, Prosperous, Wealthy, Curse-Breaker, Repairer of The Breach, Blessed, Favored, Strong, Accepted, Pretty, Diamond, Jewel, Capable, Winner, Aligned, Protected, Advancer, Influencer, Empowered, Motivated, Joy, Peace, Happiness, Decided, Clarity, Wisdom, Knowledge, Glory Carrier, Shaker, Mover, Wells of Living Waters, Secure, Present, Legacy Carrier, Purpose-Led, Fruitful, Covered, Renewed, Honored, Overcomer, Achiever, Promise Receiver!

I Am All That God Says

My Identity Is Truth & Anchored In God!
Daily Decrees
I decree that I am seated and walk in my full promise!
I decree that the promise keeper is faithful to provide over my life!
I decree abundance of rivers and abundant life is my portion.
I decree that all that belongs to me comes forth perfectly over my life.
I decree that wealth, success, abundance and my full inheritance belong to me.
The wave of more than enough finds me and locates me now through my limitless Father.
I decree my coast is enlarged and every rainbow of blessing is released now.
I pray you were blessed & generational blessings will flow through your life.
You Can See More Products @ tespeaks.com

TIFFANY EALY

#TESpeaks

www.ingramcontent.com/pod-product-compliance
Lightning Source LLC
Chambersburg PA
CBHW031300290426
44109CB00012B/665